Colours of Spring

photography by John A. Howells

poems by Gill Kingsland

Cover design by Anna Reith © Frith Books 2016
Original photography by John Howells

10 9 8 7 6 5 4 3 2 1
First Edition

Published in the United Kingdom by Frith Books

First Printing, 2016

ISBN: 1530896231
ISBN-13: 978-1530896233

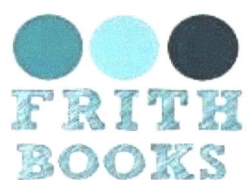

www.frithbooks.com

CONTENTS

INTRODUCTION

This volume is the product of a collaboration between a photographer and a wordsmith which, under the title *Colours of Spring*, was first exhibited as a multimedia endeavour in April 2016 at Killerton House in Broadclyst, Devon, courtesy of The National Trust.

The present volume includes all the poems and photographs from that exhibition (which were taken in the grounds at Killerton and its environs, and in part inspired by the beautiful surroundings of the estate), plus some additional material that has not been seen before.

We hope that both those familiar with the exhibition and new readers alike will enjoy accompanying us on this journey through the wonder and excitement of spring.

PREFACE

by John A. Howells

In spring, the start of the year, the world wakes up from its winter slumber. Colour returns one petal at a time, bringing the shadows to life like magic.

Finding this springtime enchantment, discovering the beauty of every flower, can be a challenge but trying is a joy in itself and to succeed, at least in part, is as exciting and rewarding as finding a precious jewel tucked into a hedgerow.

For me, as a photographer and artist, to experience spring is an annual thrill, a recurring and much anticipated delight. As much as I love all the seasons, there is a special wonder in seeing bare twigs and barren earth burst into delicate life.

Sharing my personal magical moments of this amazing season has been a special privilege; having my images studied by someone else, for them to be inspired and to bring forth beautiful poetry - like the flowers from a bare but promising branch - that is a rare pleasure for me and one that I will always treasure.

Please look through these images, read these poems, experience each glorious moment of springtime in image and in text - we hope you will enjoy each and every one of them as much as we did.

Until next year,

John Howells (Photographer and Artist)

and

Gill Kingsland (poet)

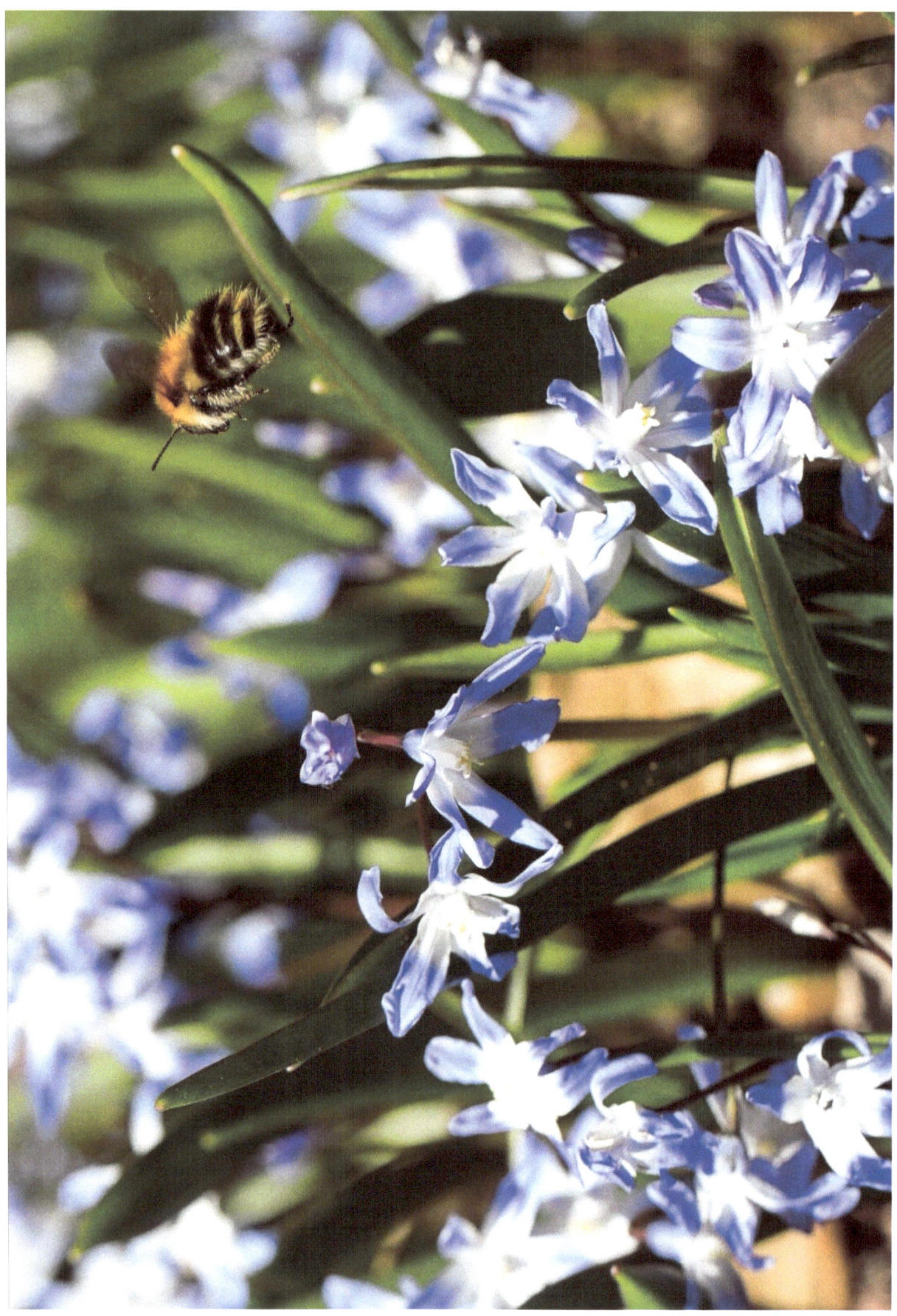

SCILLA AND THE BEE

The Bee visits,
More important than ever we know,
In the slow
Circles of Time
In which Mankind can grow.
Here the scilla,
Massed purples and delicate white
And slender green leaves,
Sustains
And attains
pollination for nectar
But in the depths dusted gold by new suns
As life evolved
Revolved
The bee's seed
Grew into Man
And Man's own circle began to spin
And will
Until
Man destroys that which nourishes life
And thus all will cease – with Scilla, and the Bee.

The San people of the Kalahari Desert tell of a bee that carried a mantis across a river. The exhausted bee left the mantis on a floating flower but planted a seed in the mantis's body before it died. The seed grew to become the first human. [http://beelore.com/2008/09/26/the-creation-story-from-the-san-people/]

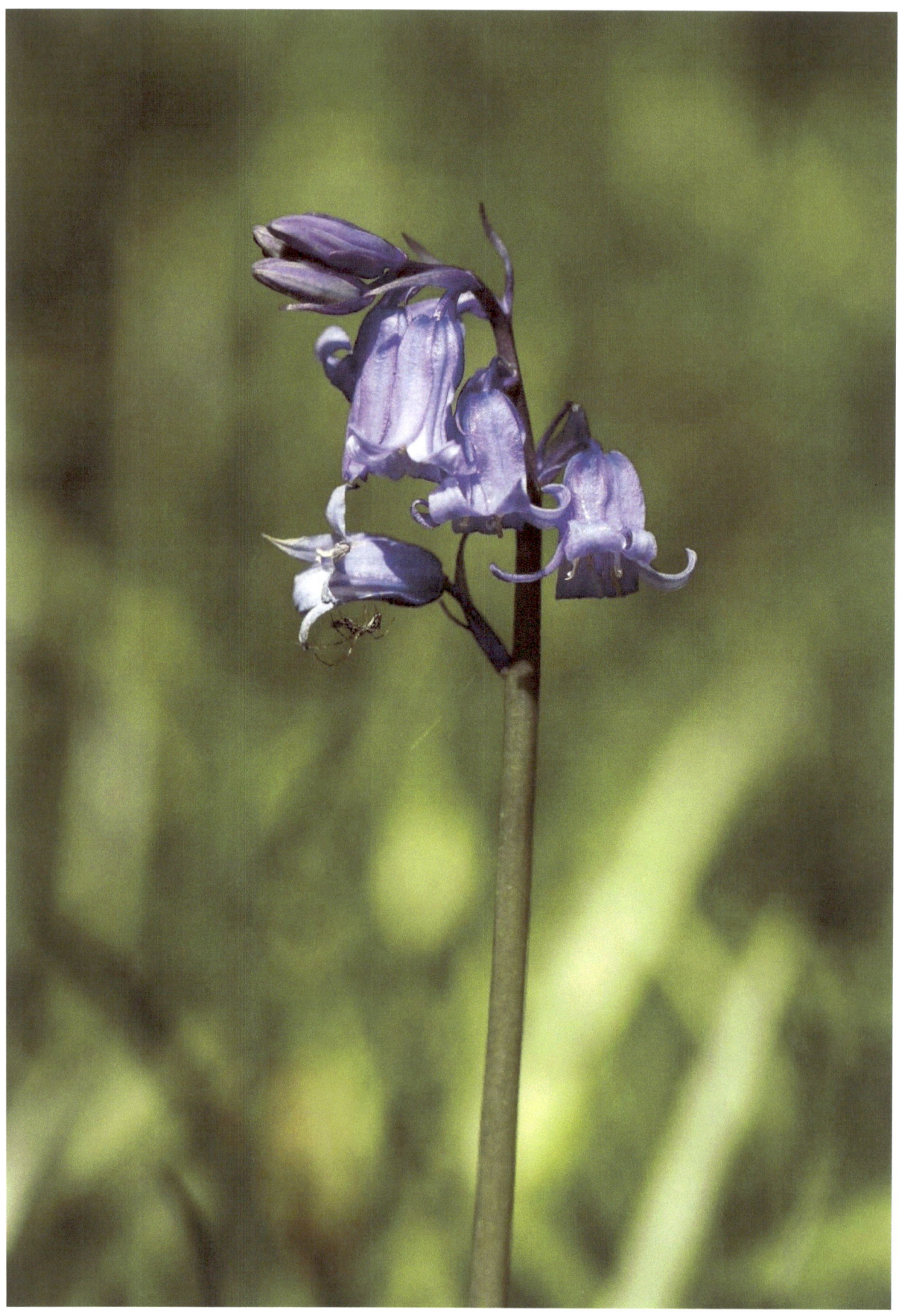

BLUEBELLS

Standing tall, the ring of bells
On the Guardian spire
Gleam in the sunshine of a spring day
But legend will say
That should danger threaten, the beat
From those throats of blue
Will bring
The fairy, the fey folk
With spears of ill-luck
To pierce the heart of the Trampler,
The remorseless killer
Of tender stems
Or the stealer of blooms
In the heart of the bluebell wood.

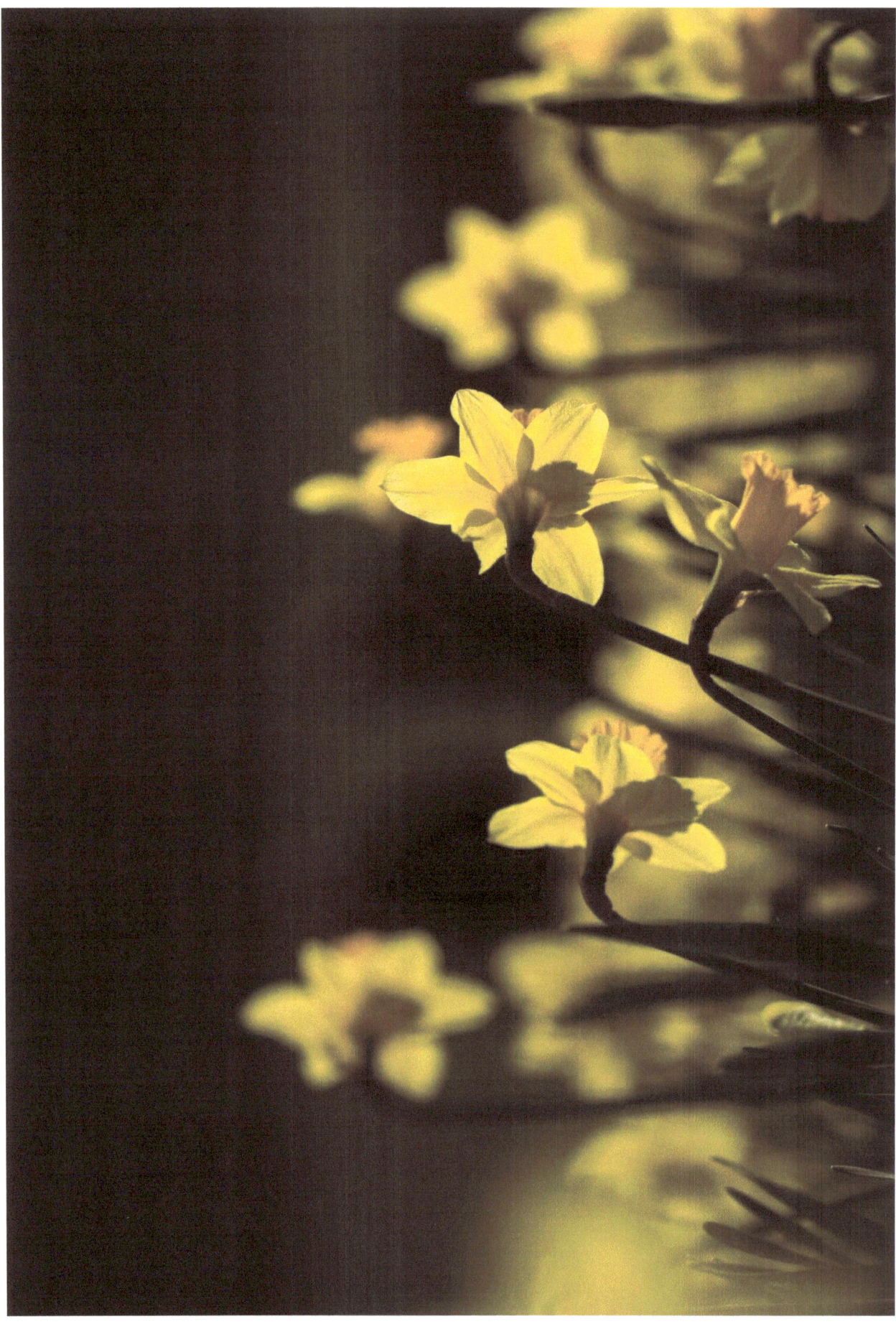

DAFFODILS

Asphodelus in the sunshine, trumpets turning to the light
Imagine then the azure seas
Of summer
And those warmed and yellow sands
As the molten beams of springtime
Spread sun-bright
At our feet
So the moment glows in memory
And spreads as gold across the lands
It's promise
That whatever else may happen
Whatever else we do
…the sun will always shine
when I am there with you…

*The flower symbolism associated with the daffodil is regard, unrequited love, chivalry, sunshine, respect and 'the sun shines when I'm with you. '

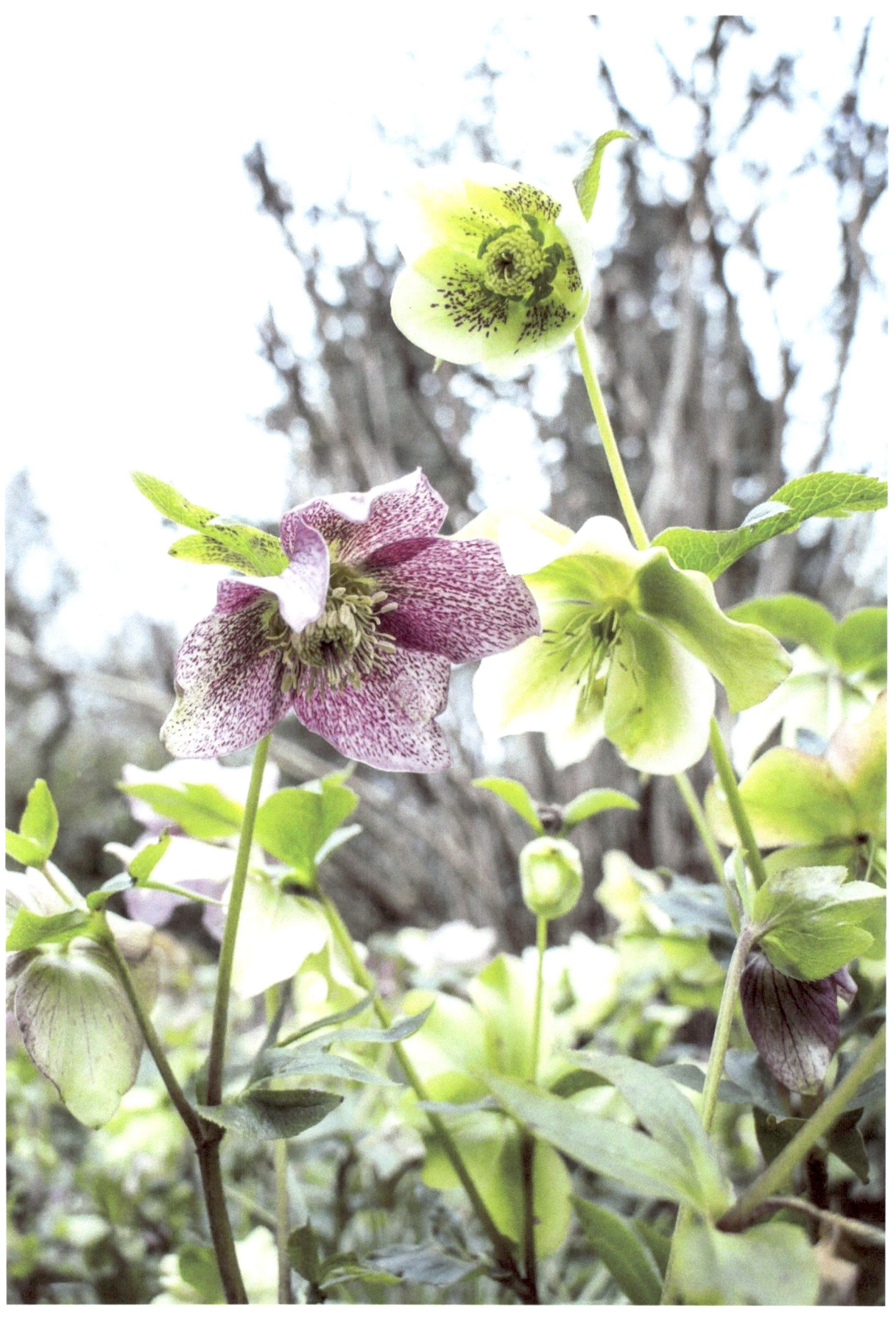

HELLEBORES

Elegant in springtime dress,
Stately
(But confess -
Sometimes a little shy
She will sigh
Behind a leaf.)
Yet she is handsome
Standing tall
In fashions' chosen colours
Ready for the pre-spring ball
But there is both beauty sweet
And bitterness
Within the Hellebore

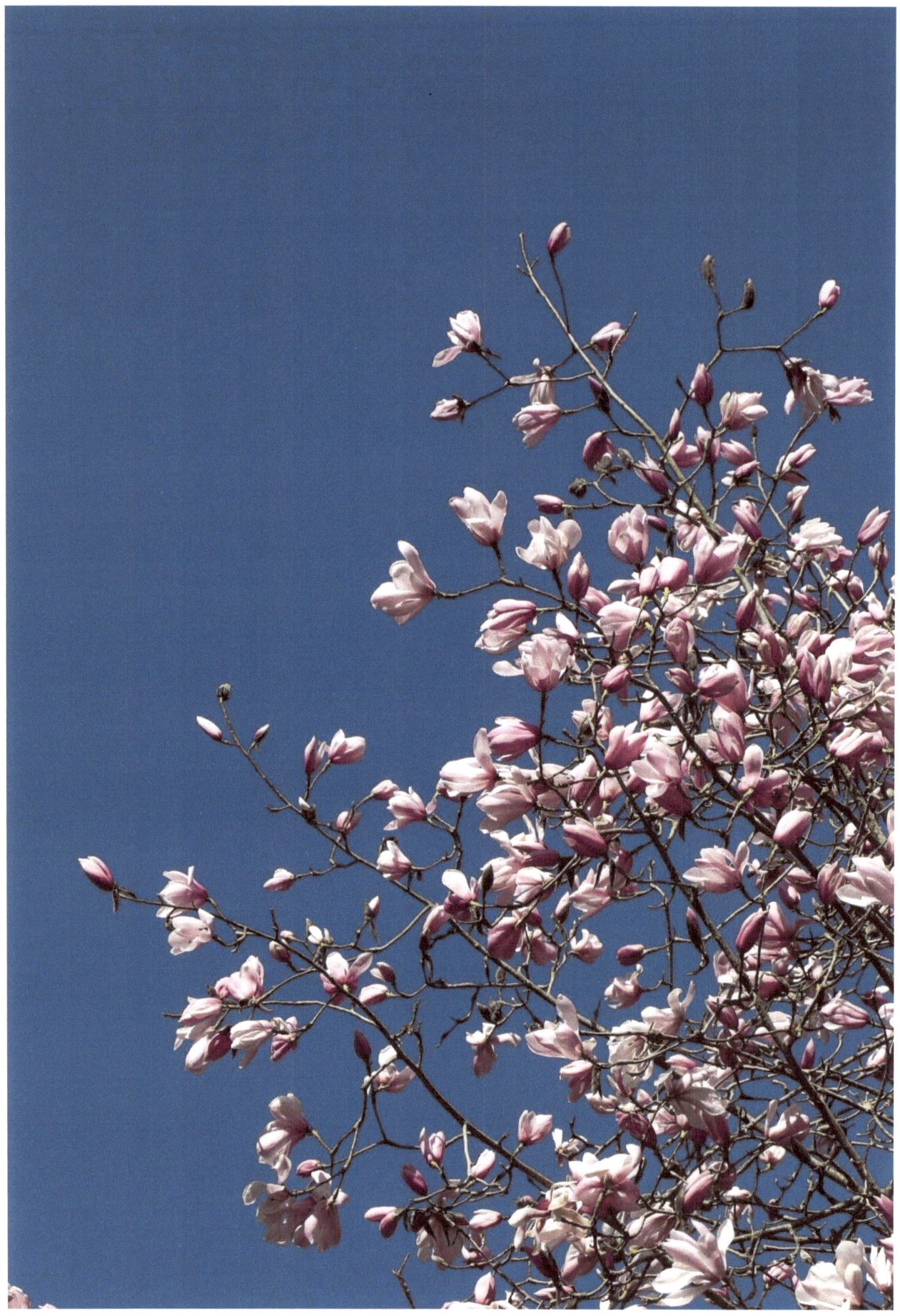

MAGNOLIA, POISED

Magnolia, vibrant pink against a faultless blue
Like butterflies clouding on a waiting branch
To rest,
Poised,
Best dressed,
Delicate,
Shown in their fullest beauty
Against a vibrant zaffre sky.

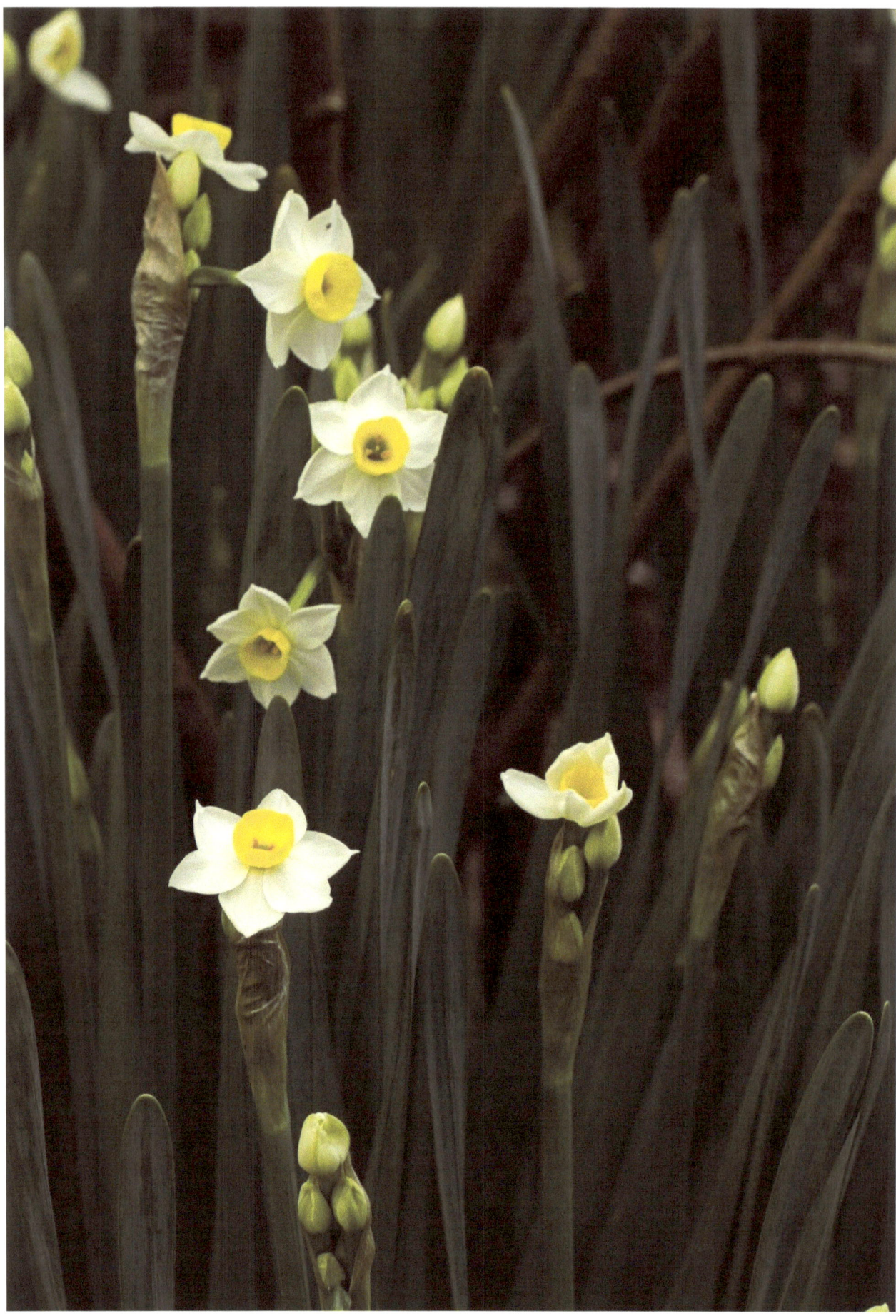

NARCISSI

Perfectly sculpted,
Perfectly shaped.
Delicate of petal,
Greenly draped.
She is palely beautiful of face
Her slenderness burgeoning
With life and grace.
Pregnant with bud
Pregnant with flower
Narcissi
Clustered in a springtime bower.

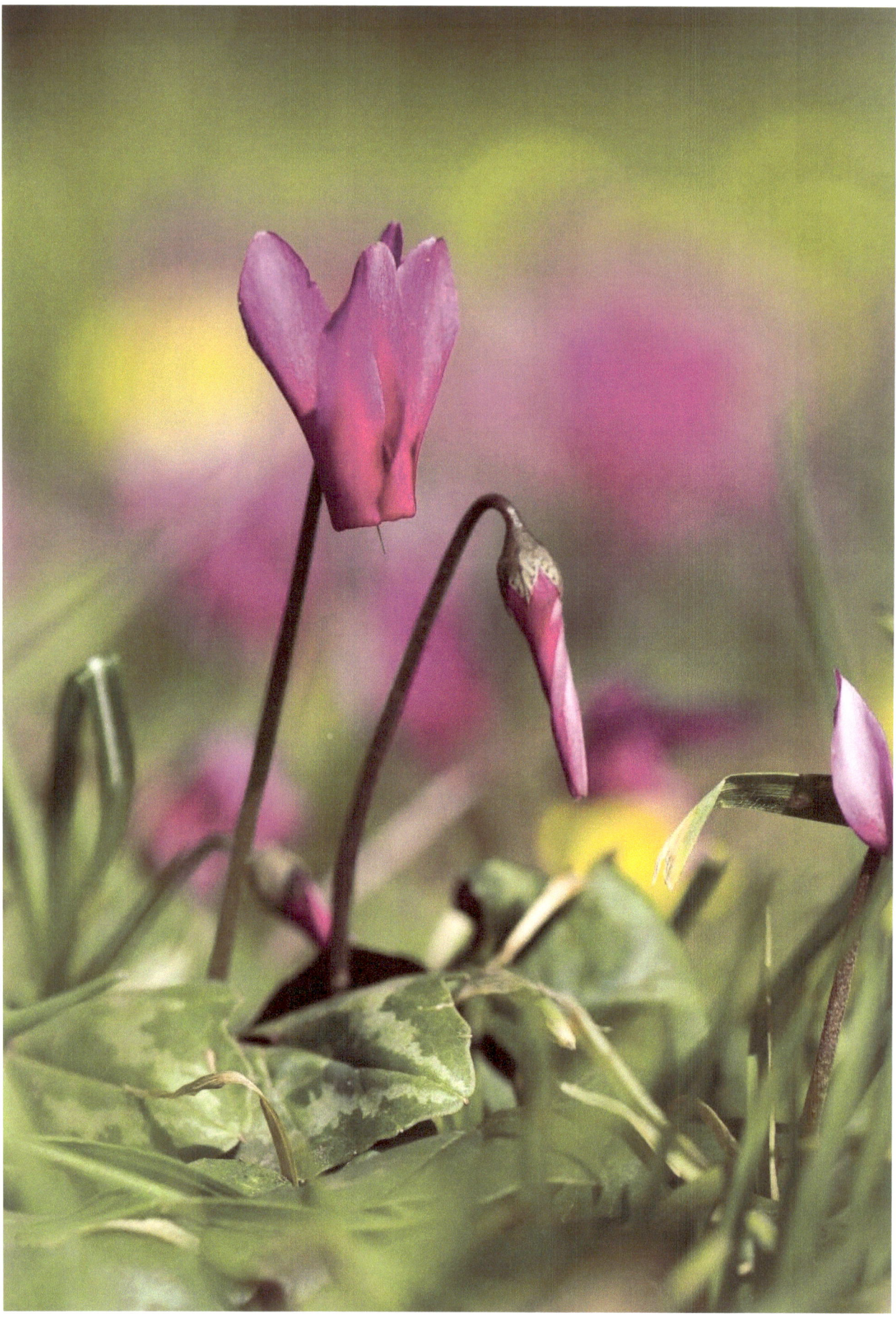

CYCLAMEN

Under the hem of Winter's cloak
Cyclamen trembles
As the cold, chill air warms to Spring's first light touch
And she bids farewell to the sterner season of ice.
Now, as the land prepares to soak
In the golden warmth
Of Spring's delight,
Winters' flowers
Stretch outwards into the bright
Greening spaces
And sunlit places
To take their ease.

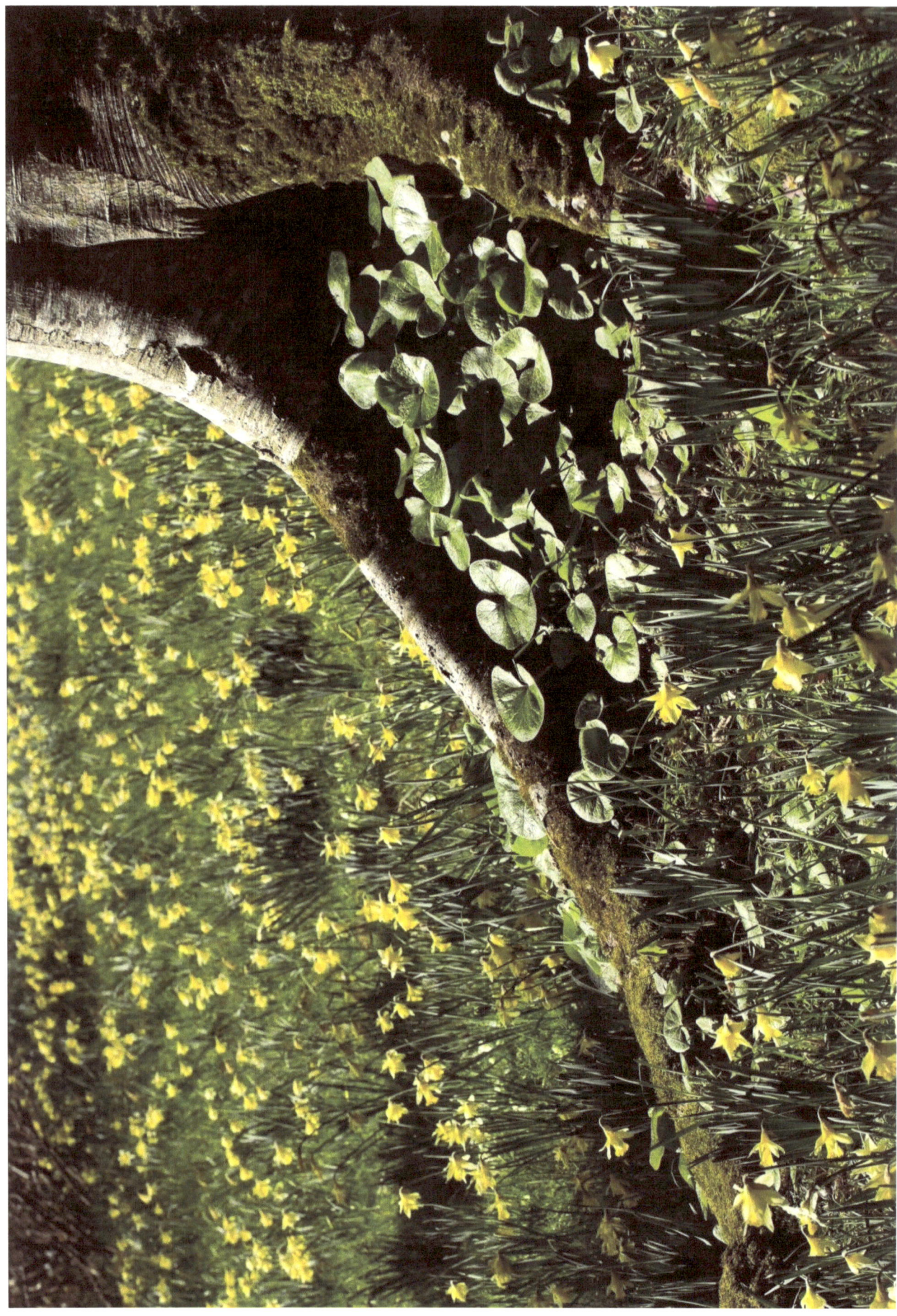

EMBRACED IN TIME AND PLACE

The Seasons circle, just the same:
Summer. Autumn, Winter, Spring
Whatever we call them, whatever the name.
But – as circles within circles – there is Time
That moves for some at a different pace.
Held safe
In a close embrace
By rooted arms
The green leaves of a smaller, faster living vine
Entwine
And nestle in the hug of the slower
Timeline of, to them, a giant,
A tree.

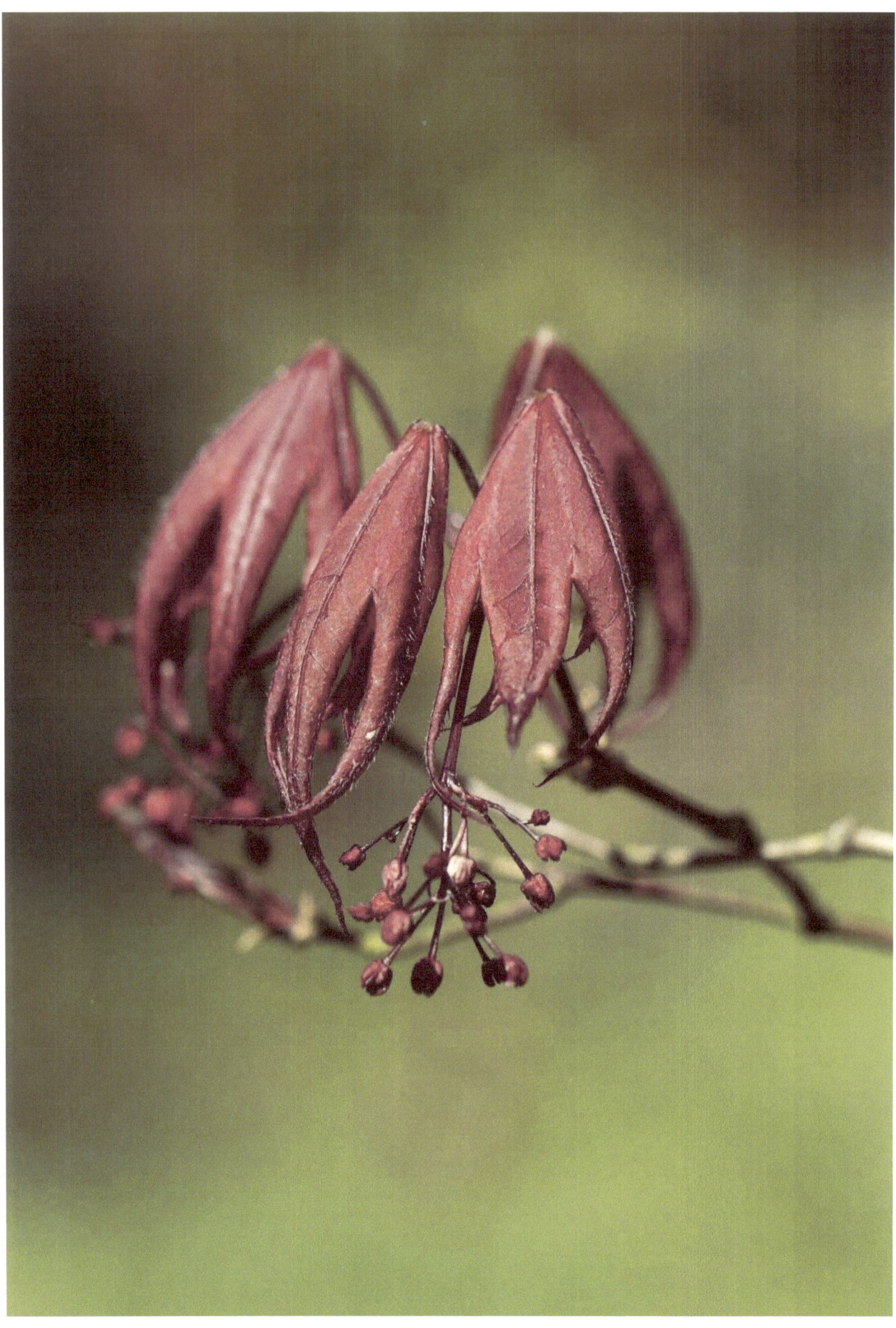

ACER

Leaf-claw, red against the growing swell of green
Glowing bright
She knows she's seen
Berried seedings hanging low
As the seasonal tide will ebb and flow
And as the world spins
Around the sun's molten pall
She turns smaller circles at its call.

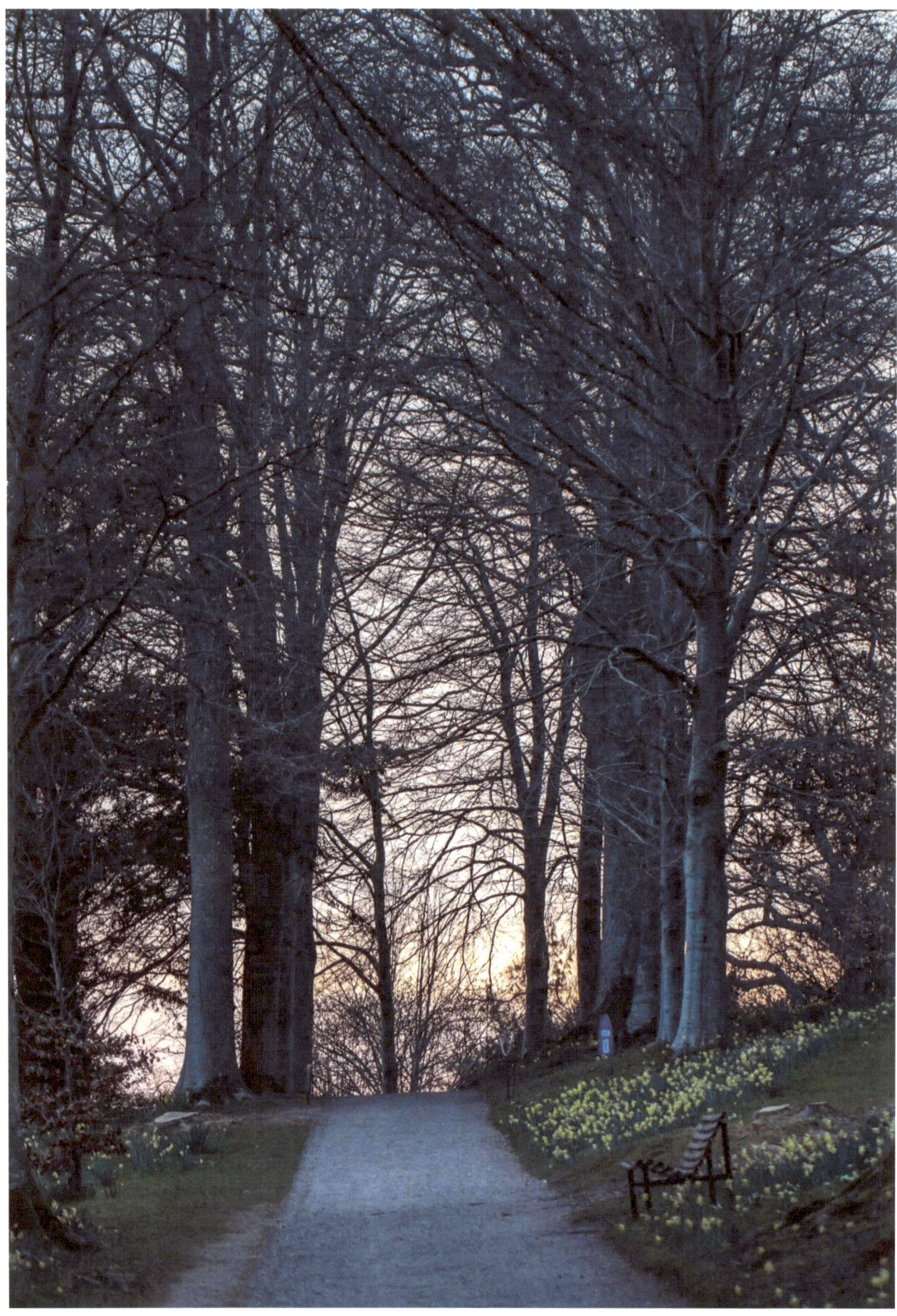

BEECH WALK

To step along the Beech Walk
In certain moments in the year
Is to tread the line
Of moving time
As Winter, paused in parting,
Shares a fleeting kiss
With Spring
The beech trees, stark, await their clothing
While at their feet
Her golden trumpets
Announce her chariot
And Winter's light
Takes flight
From her more delicate beauty
And burgeoning heat.

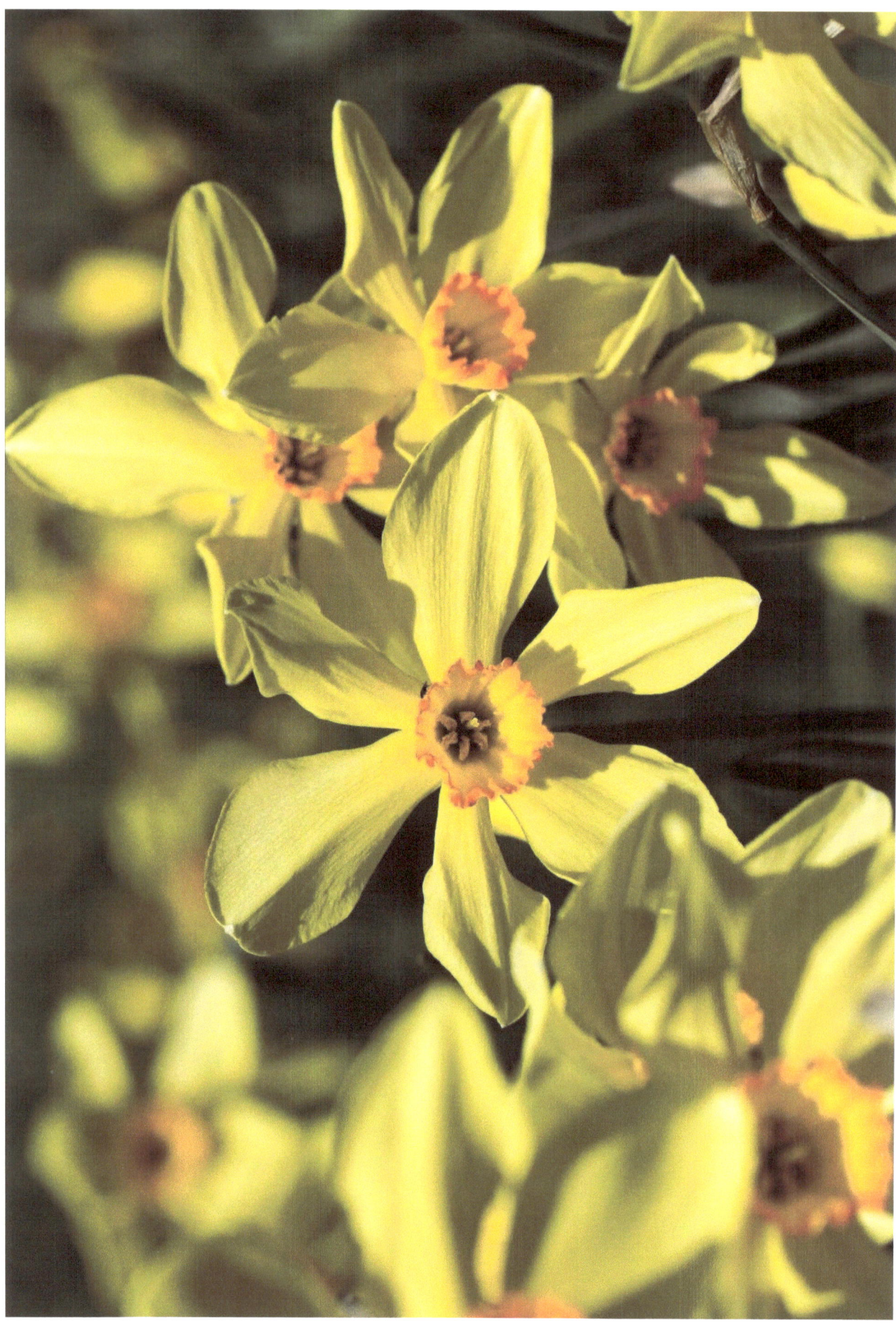

HERE'S LOOKING AT YOU

Messengers of Spring's advent
They gather
Golden, sun-kissed carpets
Bright, trumpet-clumps
They colour-clamour the message
Head bump
In the breeze,
Spring is here! Look! Look! Look!
And we look, and walk on
But the daffodil turns
To watch, not for our returning but for the path of the Sun,
Ra must rise and bless
HER returning
For in their law and learning
Without him, Spring cannot stay.

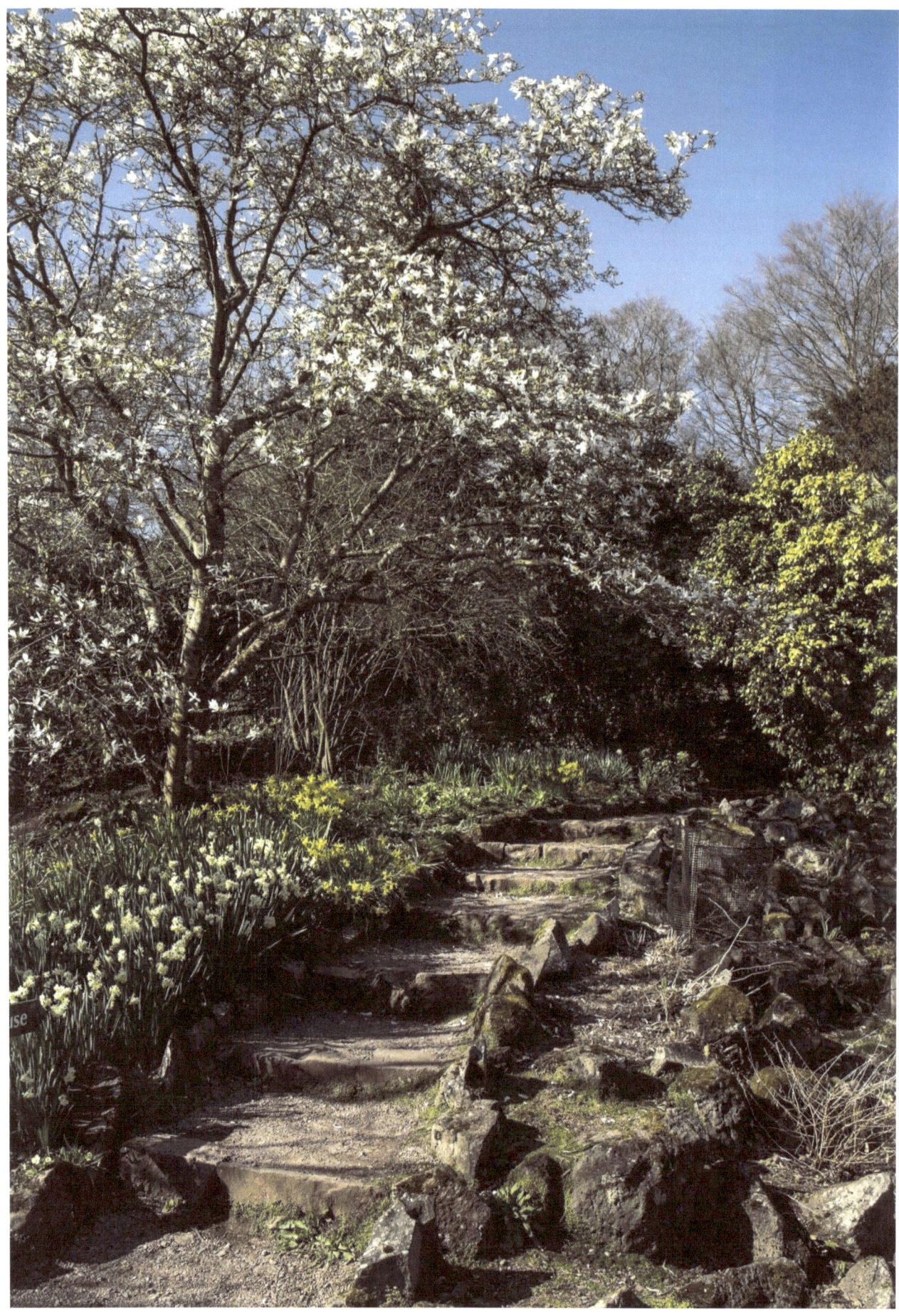

MAGNOLIA AND PATH

Gathered here, for a reason,
Clad in the rich garb of the season
Magnolia waits with her peers
Beside the stepped path of secrets
Where, as Spring passes the Summer Queen will tread.
Into the deep, dark shadows above,
Through which no soothsayers or seers
may pass
With blurred or sun-scarred eye
To make pronouncement
On the futures that lurk
Within,
And ply
Their trade of half-truth, truth or lie.

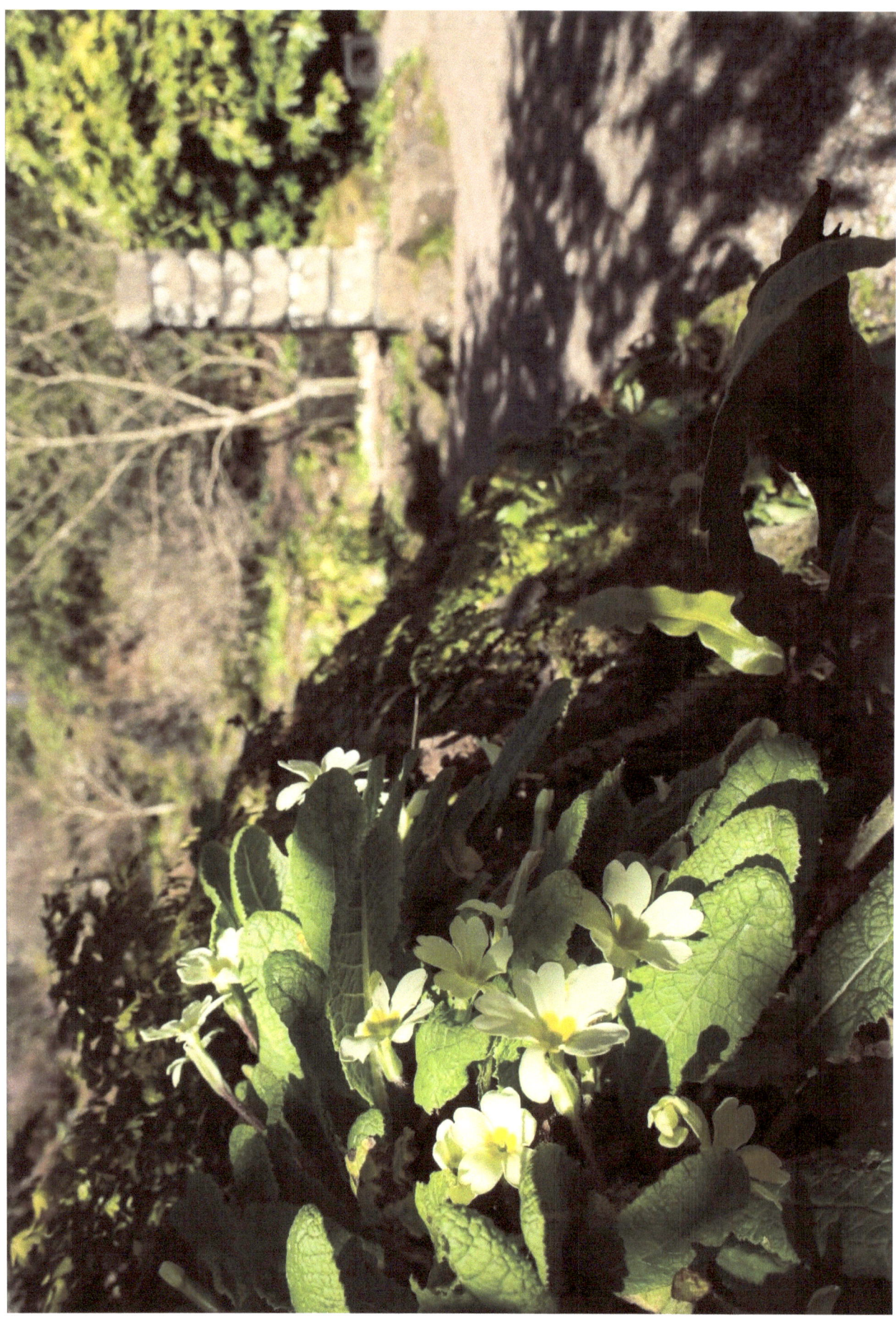

PRIMROSE AND PILLAR
GIANT'S MOORING IN THE TIDE OF TIME

In the long, long ago when the tide of time turned
And all myth and magic fled
There was a philosopher, a giant - once of the Fey
Who longed to stay
For the new day
Ahead.
He built a boat to sail the seas of time
And was carried from his home to spin
Through uncharted times of tin
Iron, steam
Streams
Of light inside a glass skin
Dizzy and lost,
He cast a line
Which held him still in a quiet time.
He planted a primrose
For the purity of this peace
And held to his mooring
Until from the chaos
Came a new day dawning.

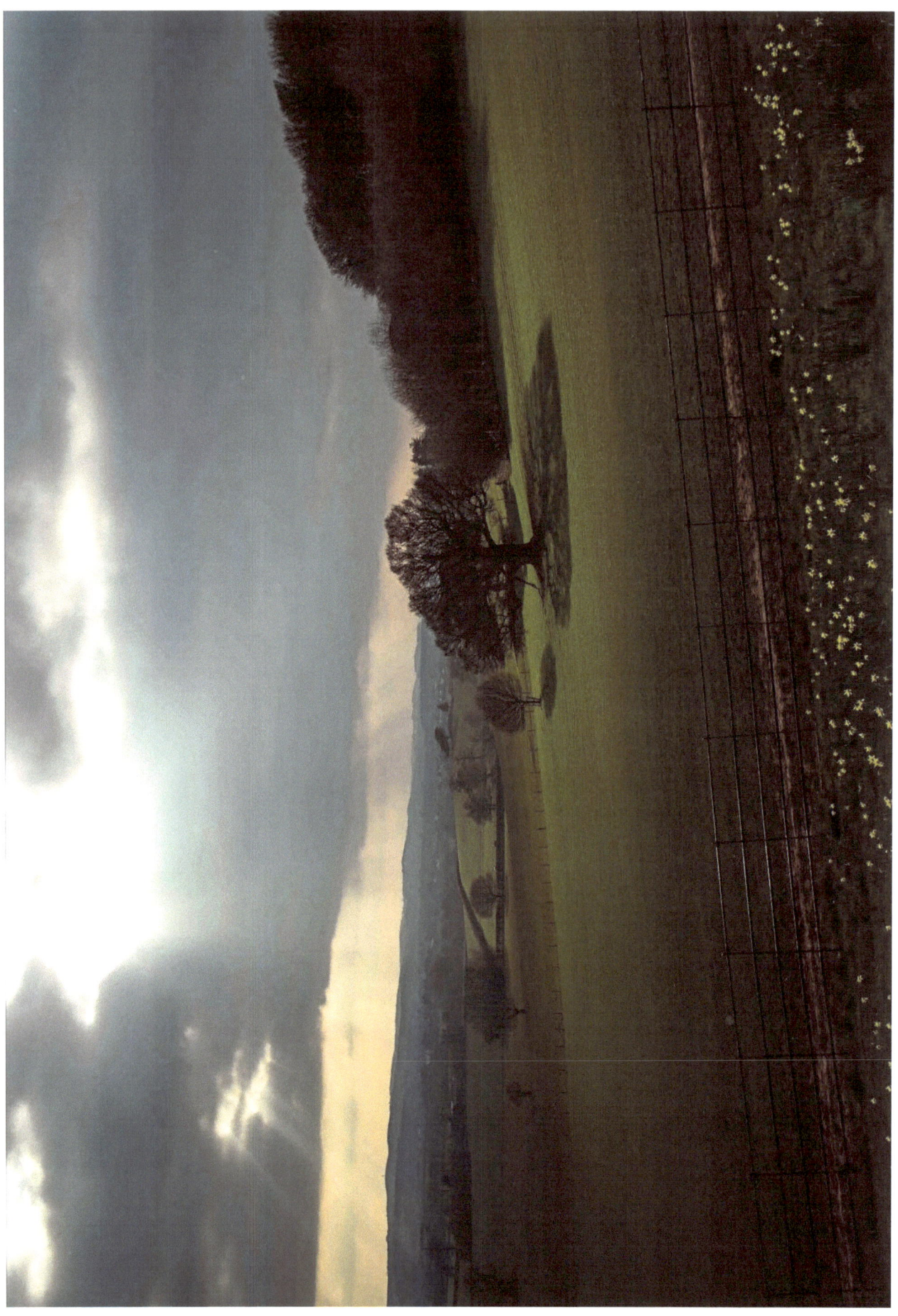

SUNBURST

While the land is wet-locked and muddy
And in the distance more rain falls
Here
Where older life, listening to Spring's calls
awaits its greening
And new life bursts with new vibrancy
A silvered light
Shines through a mercury sky
As the sun – from high
Above
Comforts the land
And awaits the arrival of the dove.

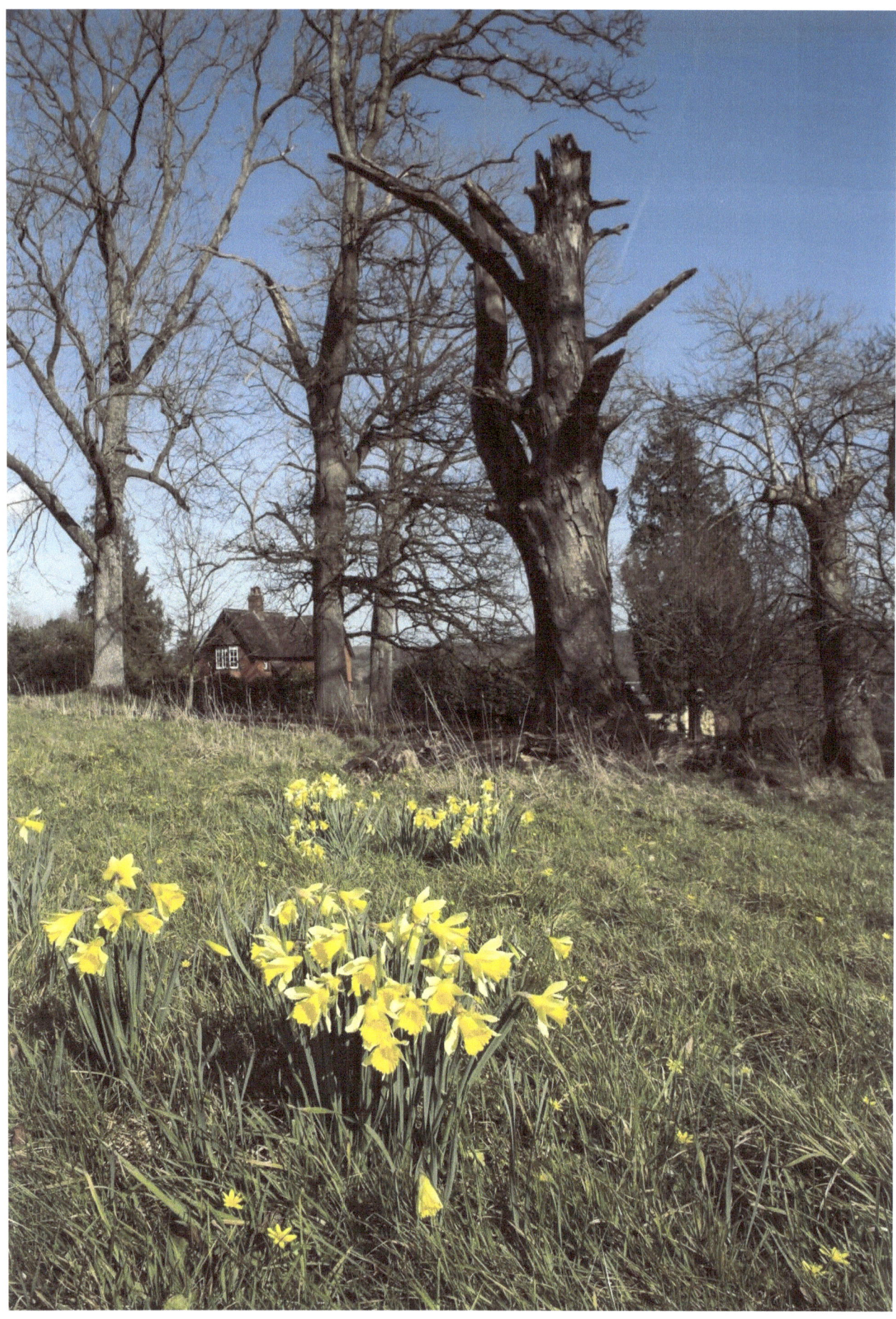

TREE AND DAFFS

In a field where other trees grow tall
One stands as if alone.
Broken, battered, not yet ready to fall
It draws the eye.
The sun dapples it
The bright blue sky enfolds it
Daffodils dip their golden trumpets at its feet
As it soaks in spring's heat
And its sap slowly rises
At the call.

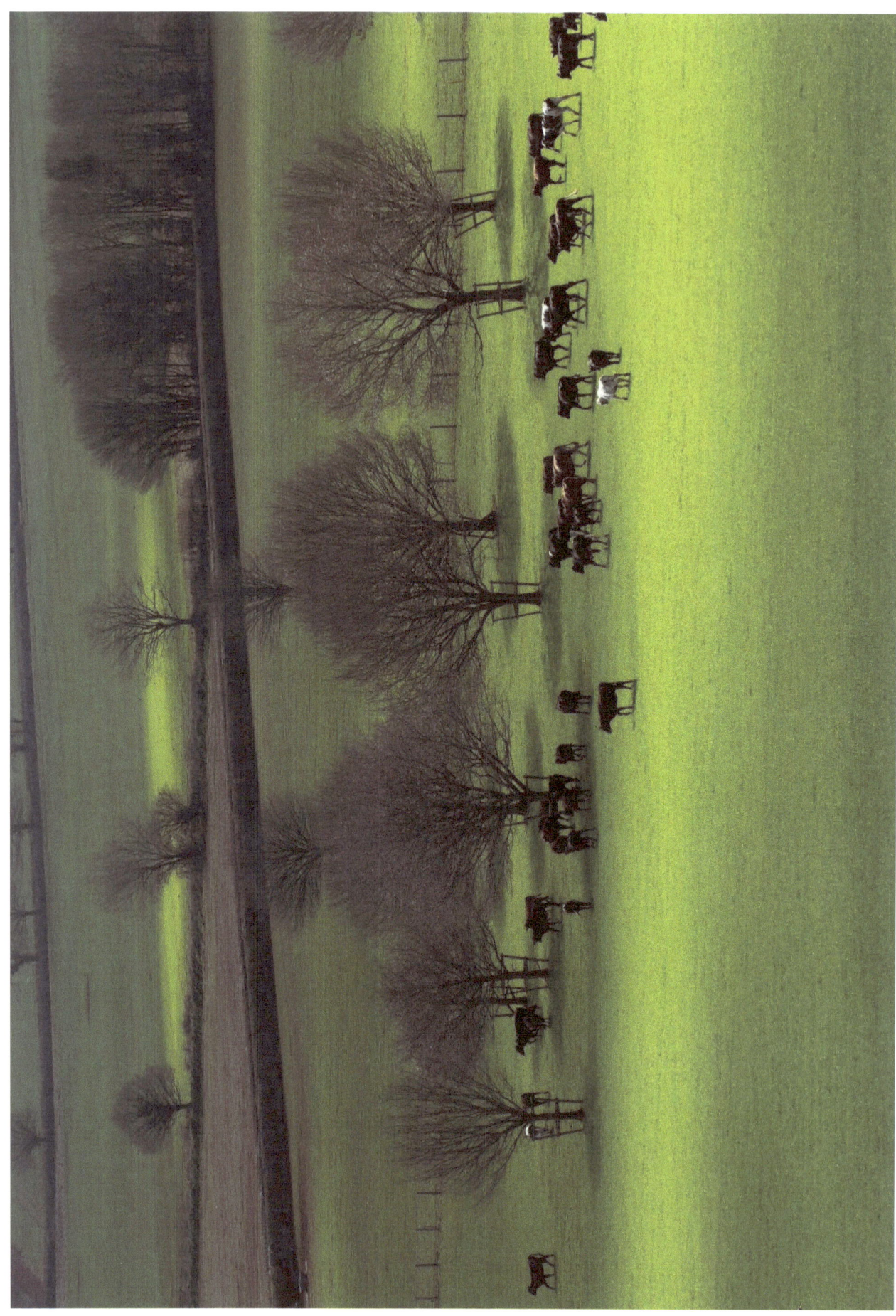

A GREEN AND PLEASANT LAND

Verdant, treed and meadowed
Where varied herds graze
In the morning haze
And through the hours to dusk
Where birds in branches sing
In joyful chorus
And the land, greenly porous
Soaks up rain,
Steams under the sun
And lays such rich soil
Over the bones of its history,
All under the blue bowl of the sky
As time rolls by
In this green and pleasant land.

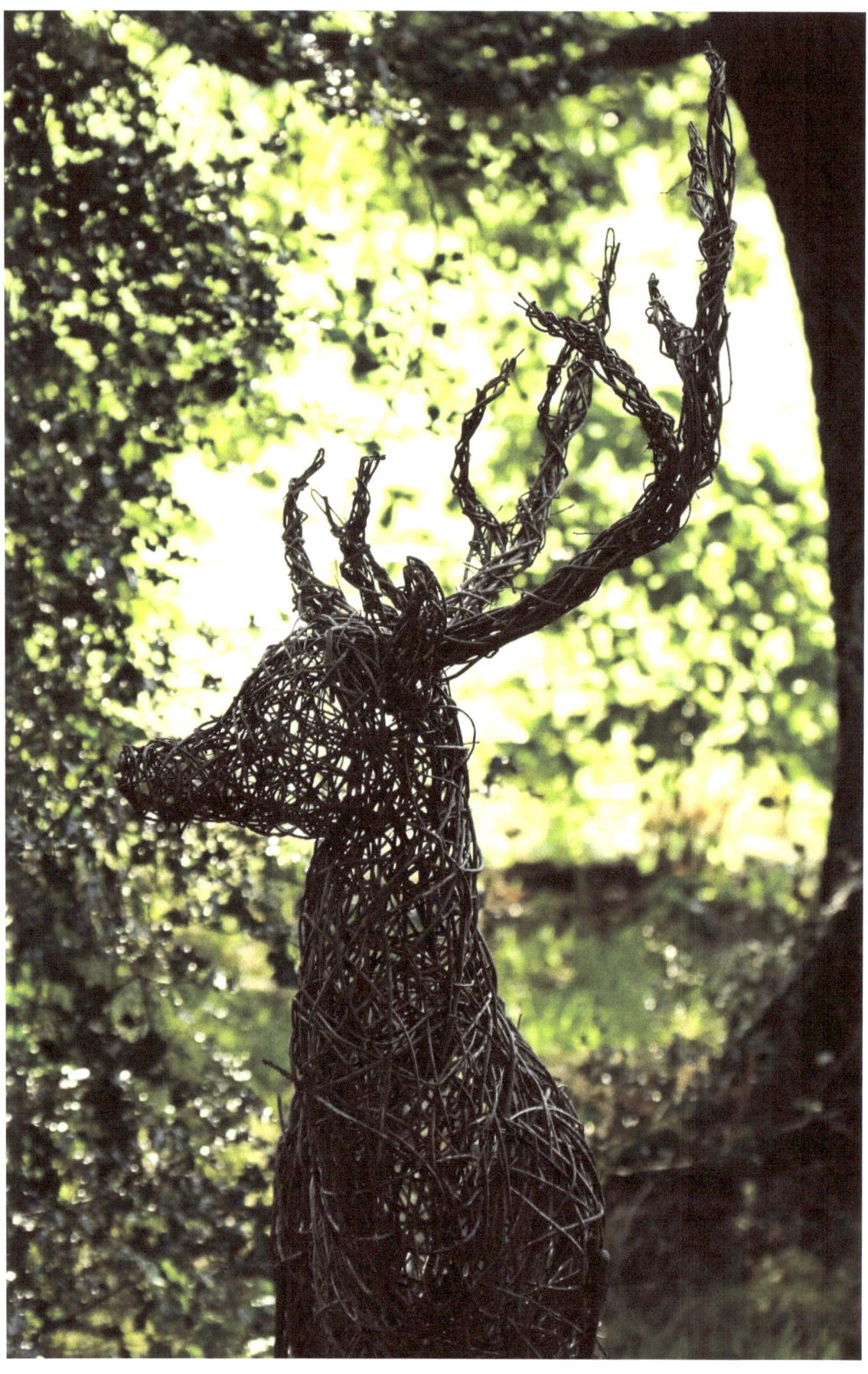

THE STAG

In the forest, of the forest
Head held high
As around the trees bow and sigh
And small creatures use him as climbing frame home or host
Willow-woven
Hazel framed
Forever still, forever poised
Held with the pride
Of Every Stag
Watching over
Every Doe
Every Fawn
Every seasonal bride.
The Stag.

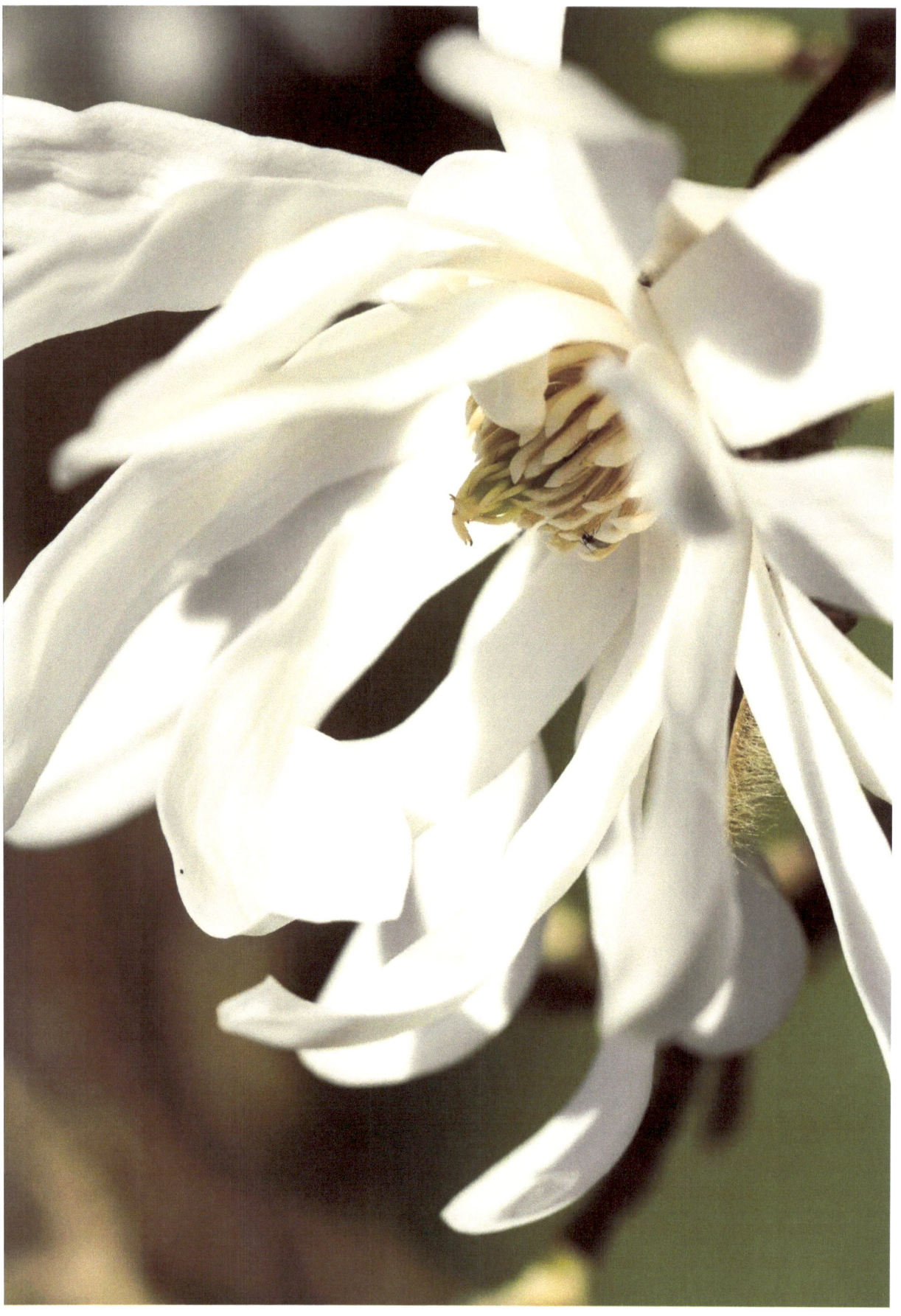

WHITE MAGNOLIA

With tangled purity,
Still wearing a wedding dress
That is less
Pristine
Now that it has seen
The party
Magnolia
Reaches out
To take the next step
Another whirl about
The dance floor
Before
Life is reaffirmed and recreated.

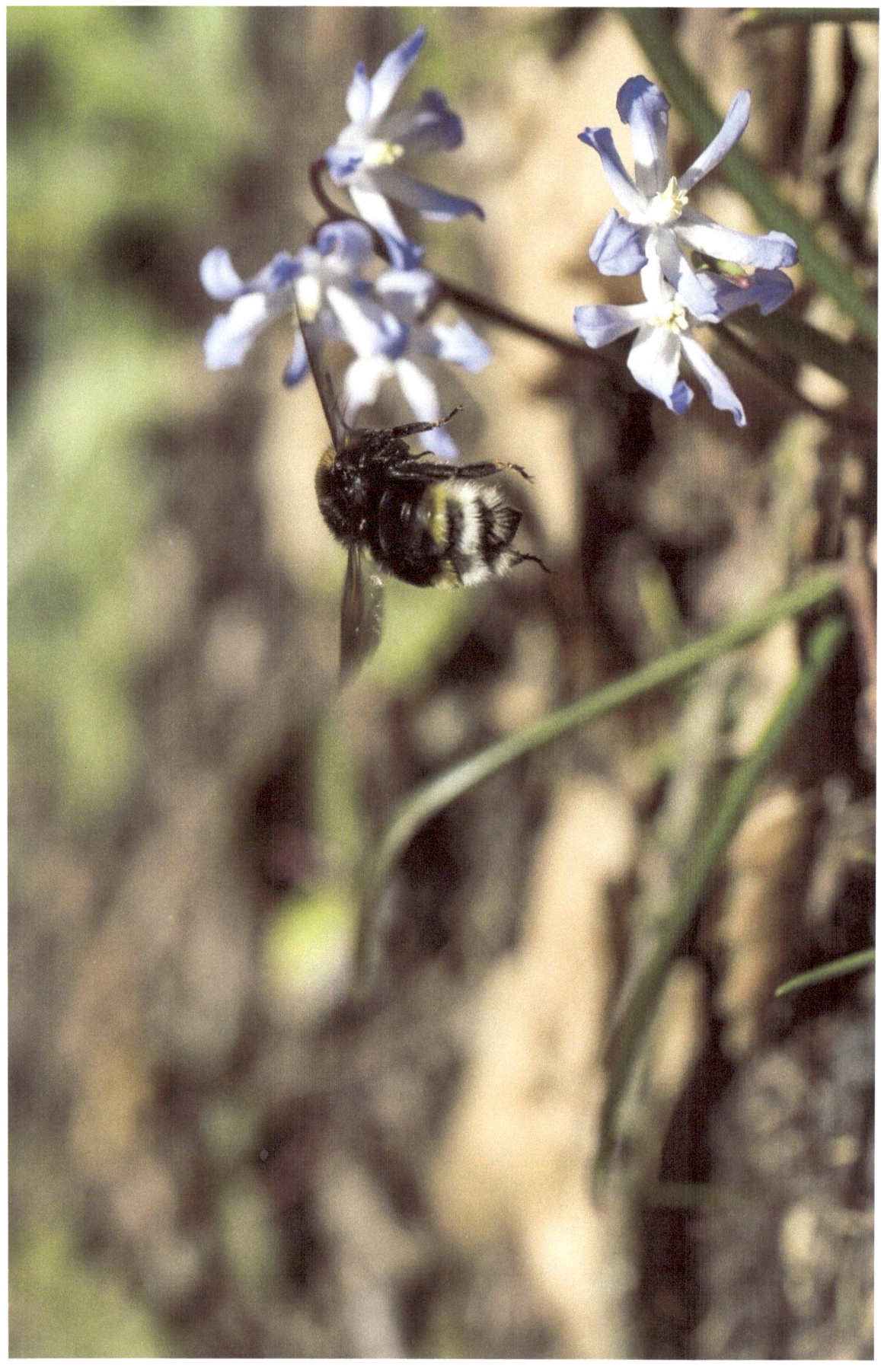

SCILLA AND THE BEE'S KISS

Neglected, slightly apart
Alone at the start
Not invited to join the party
This single scilla flowers
At spring's behest
Brave and true
Purple with blue
She unfurls
Uncurls
And Bee sees her beauty first
So she, before all others,
Receives his kiss.

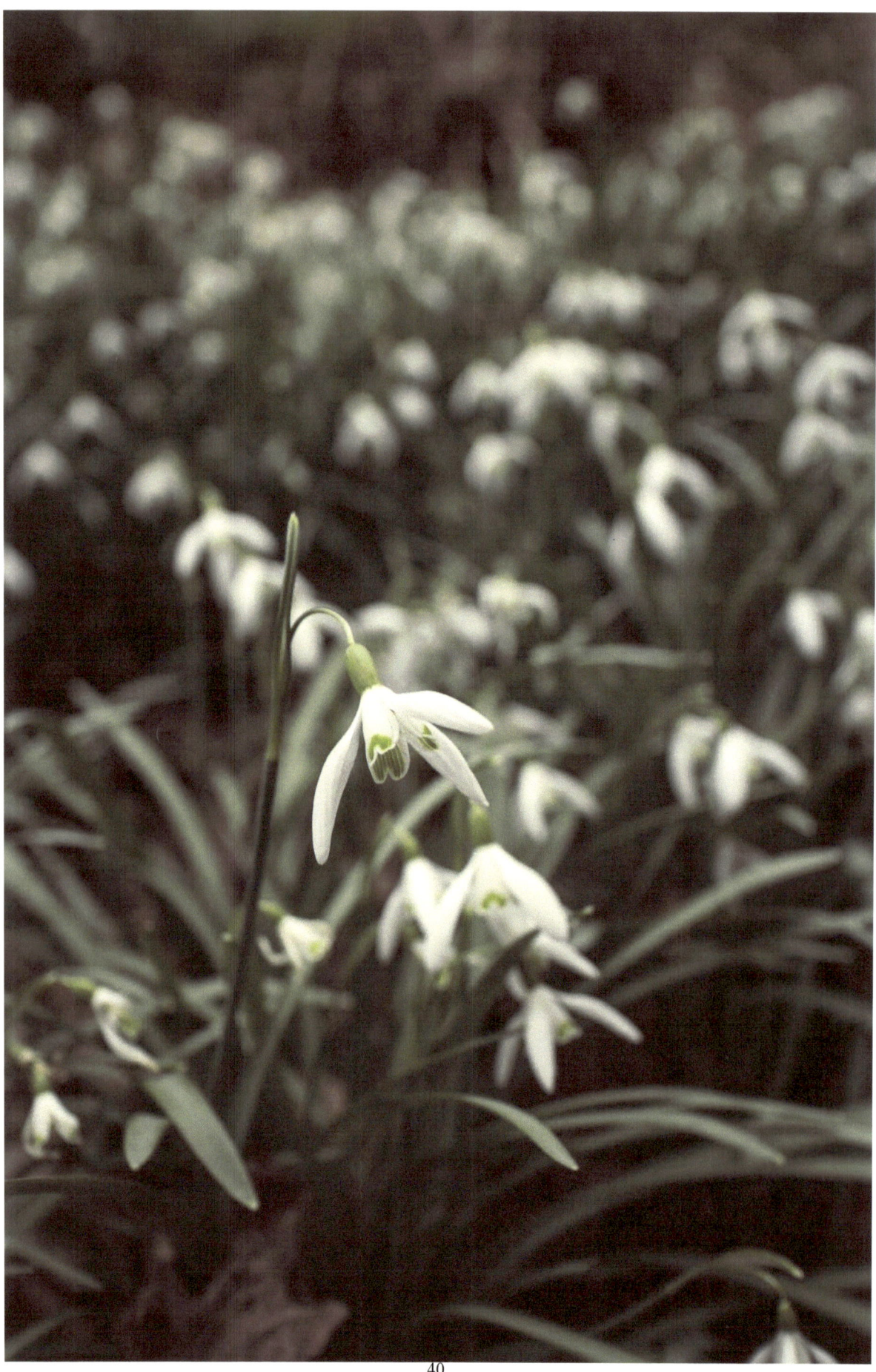

GALANTHUS

The promise of Winter's Passing
Is tucked within each bloom.
Snow White
Defies winter's doom
And reaches out a hand to Spring
In all her glory
While her own story
Hides in dales and glades
And she goes unplucked
This mythical harbinger of death
Whose pure breath
Brings
Springs
Early message
I Am Come.

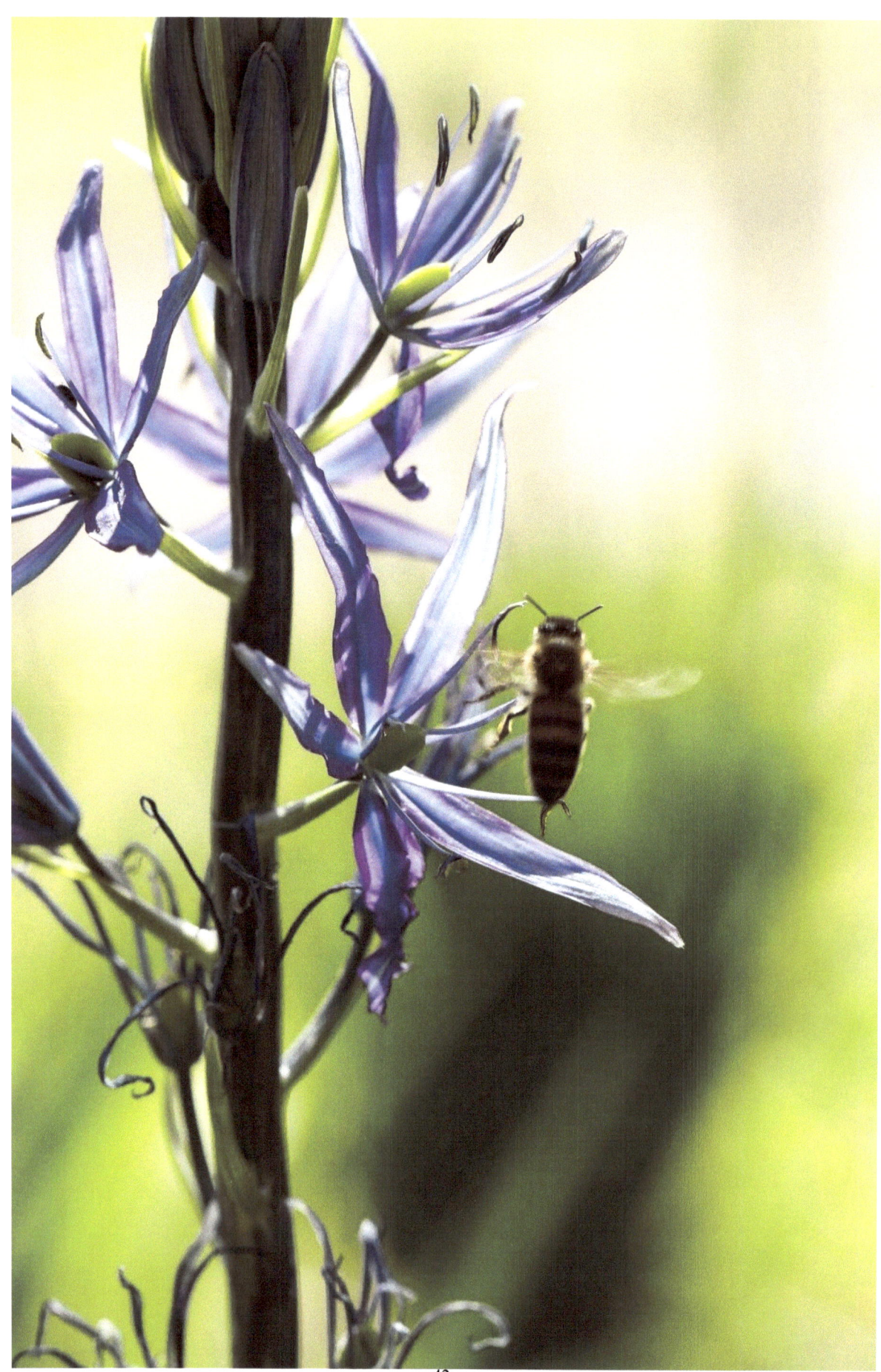

CAMASSIA

Delicate, on a sturdy pleat-topped stem
Petals made of spears of dusk
Scents of sweet musk
Fill the air

Six bladed flowerlets
Held tall
Call
And there comes Bee
To see
Each lance
And to dance
On a stage
Of lilac coloured blades
For his supper.

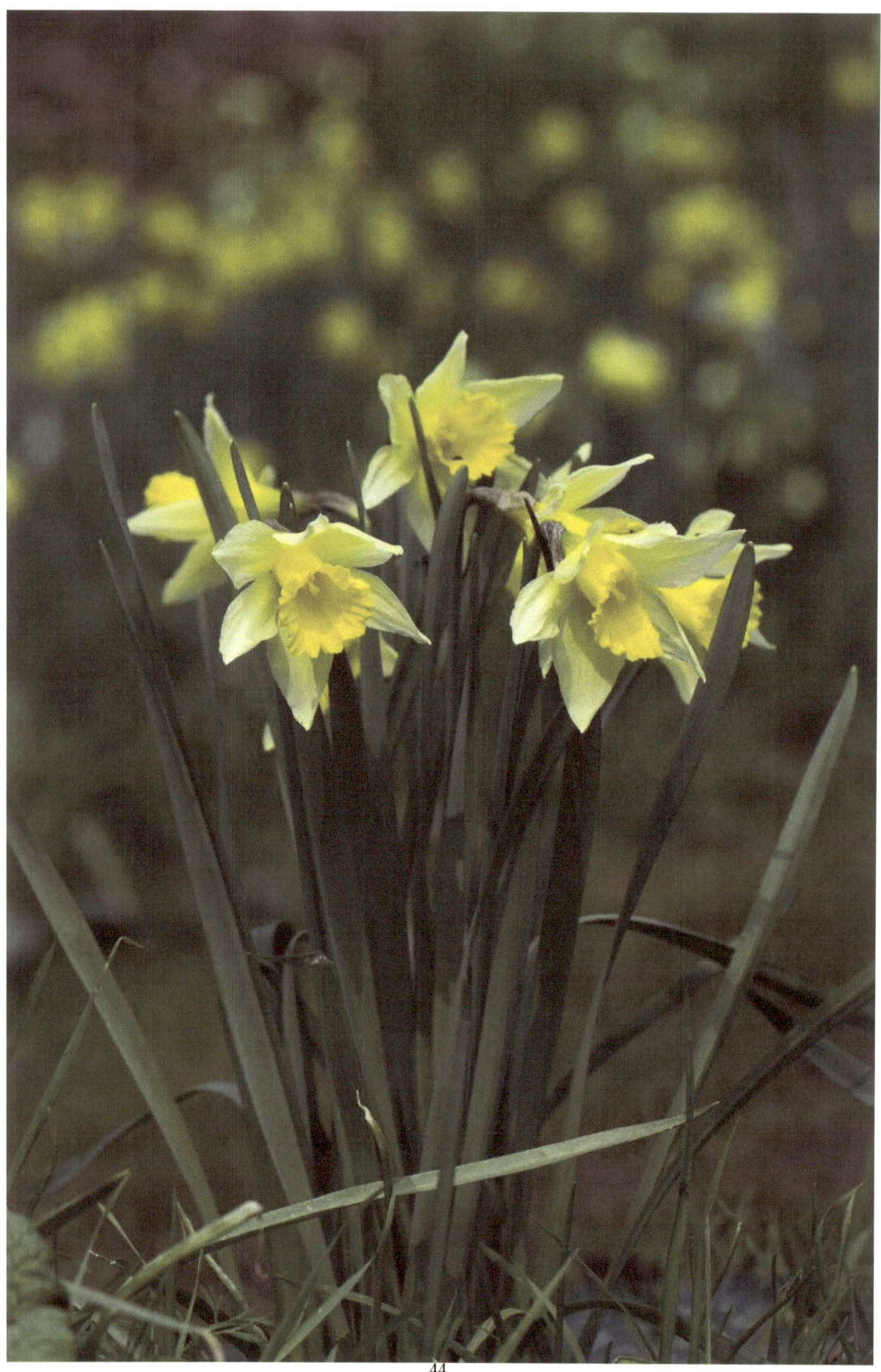

DAFFODILS AND ME

Daffodils, in a sea of yellow and green
Know they have been seen
And turn their heads towards my lens
Deciding here to be my friends
Petals frilled and stems so straight
They wait
For the inept
Meld
Of Daffodil sea, and me
Caught by, and in, a mechanical eye
Held
By man
Doing all that a mere man can
To share
The beauty of a springtime, landlocked sea
Of golden yellow
Before time moves on and they must flee
Until their next blooming.

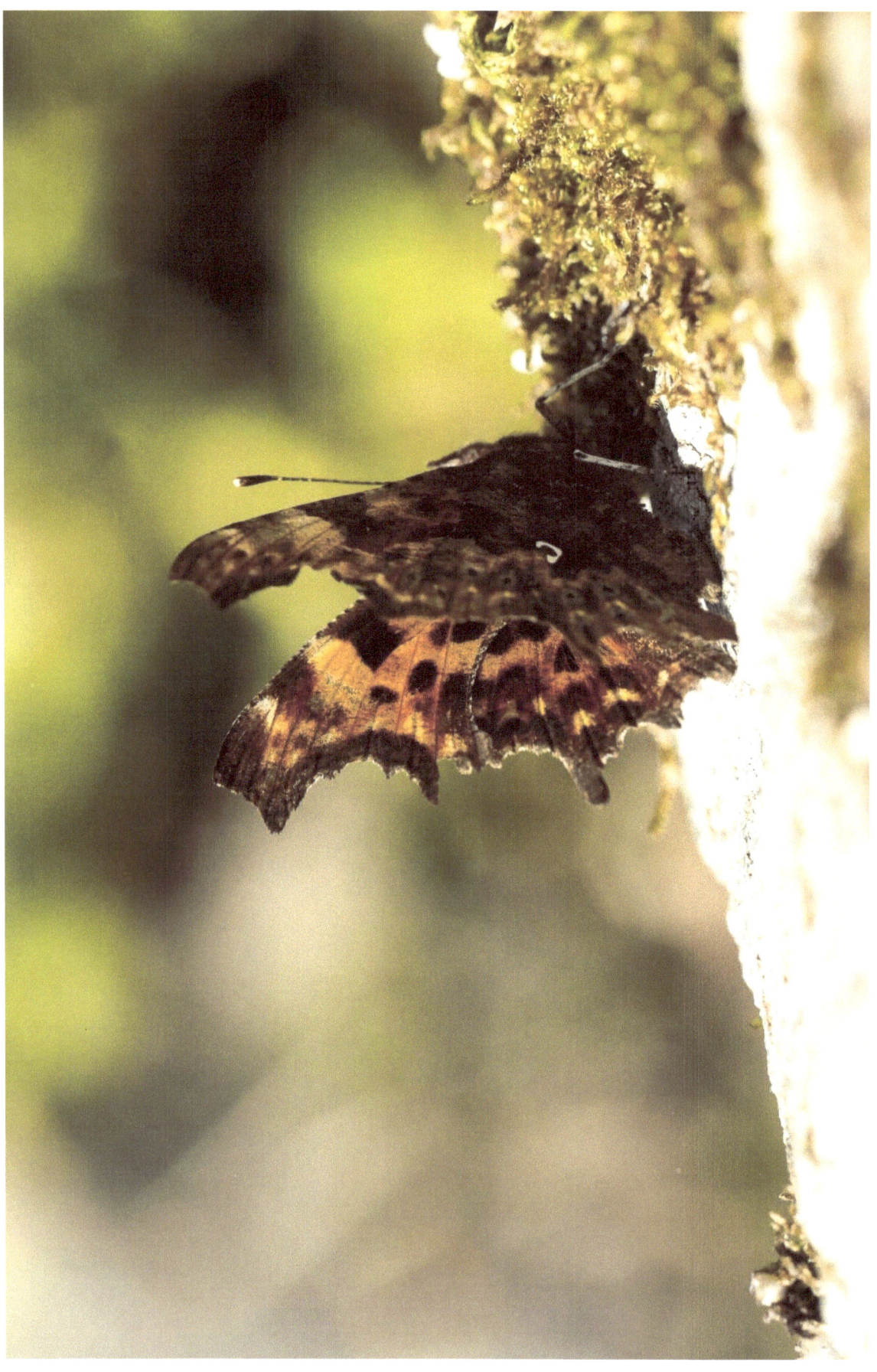

THE PUNCTUATED BUTTERFLY

Itself, a fragile creature of rare and tender beauty
A nymphalid,
Caught in sight as it dallied,
A pause between moments
A delight
A bearer on its wing
Of a certain mark
A signifier of the gasp, a breath, an instant
Poised
In the litany of it's delicate beauties
Used after the 'and'
Seen at rest on nettle, twig or land
Nature uses the much debated
Often slated
Oxford Comma.

The 'Oxford comma' is an optional comma before the word 'and' at the end of a list:
For further information http://www.oxforddictionaries.com/words/what-is-the-oxford-comma

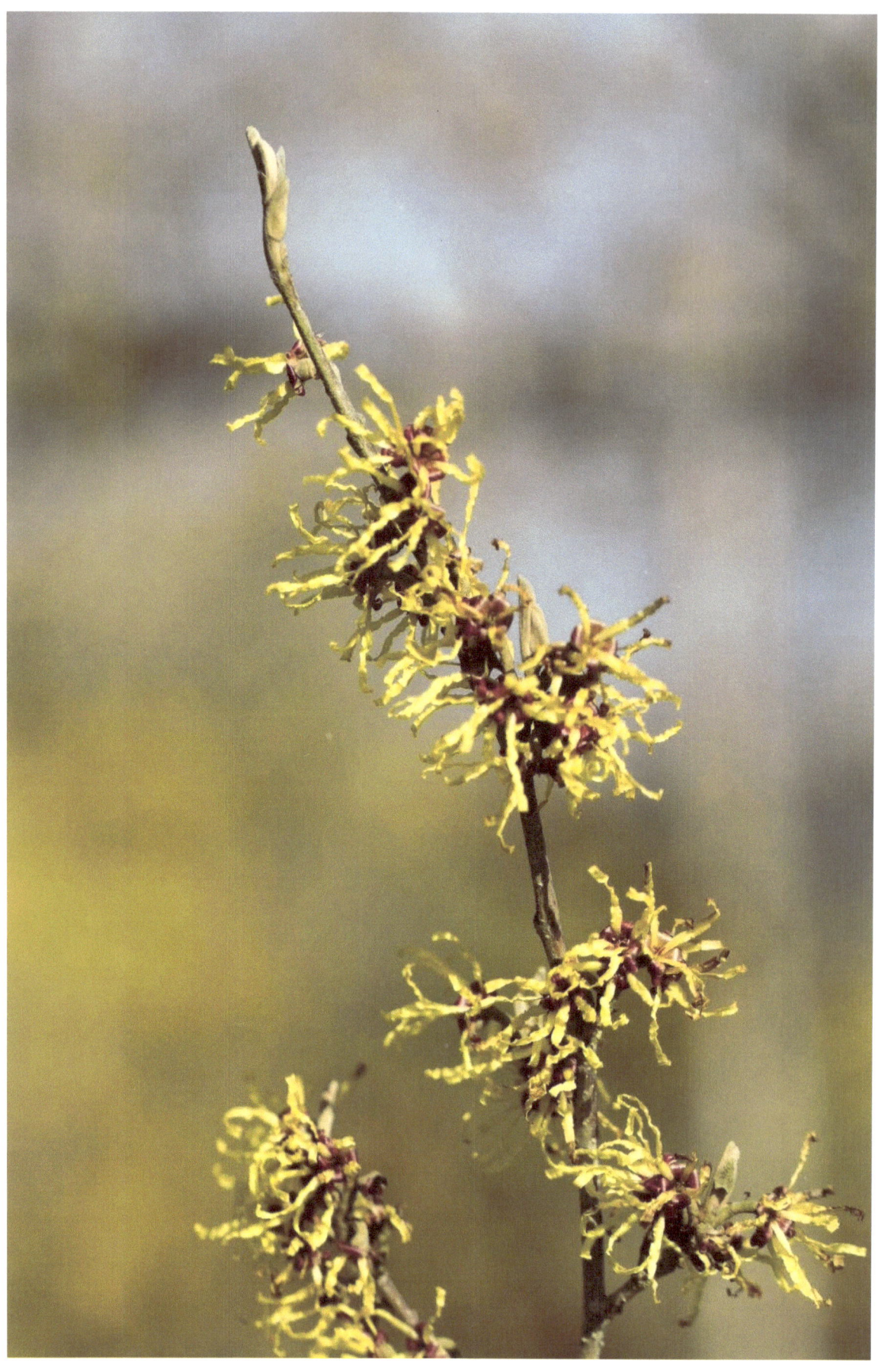

WITCH HAZEL

Some fluffed, some gnarled
On twig sticks they ride
Small buffets and dips
And wind circled slips
Each a part of a whole
That plays a role
In country care and lore
That sooths each barb and sore
The country witch
The hedgewitch
The soother of the hurt
The unburnt
Witch Hazel.

ABOUT THE AUTHORS

JOHN A. HOWELLS is a passionate photographer, naturalist, and artist. A professional wildlife photographer for over fourteen years, he finds inspiration in the flora and fauna of the beautiful Devon countryside in which he lives. John takes photographic and traditional media commissions, and runs regular photography workshops at several locations in Devon, including RHS Rosemoor and Castle Drogo.

www.johnahowells.co.uk

GILL KINGSLAND is a freelance writer, poet, and author. A teacher of creative writing for several years, she holds an MA in Studies in Fiction from the University of East Anglia, and her short stories have been published in the Academic Anglophone Society of Romania's *American, British, and Canadian Studies* journal.

www.gillkingsland.com

www.ingramcontent.com/pod-product-compliance
Lightning Source LLC
Chambersburg PA
CBHW050859180526

45159CB00007B/2727